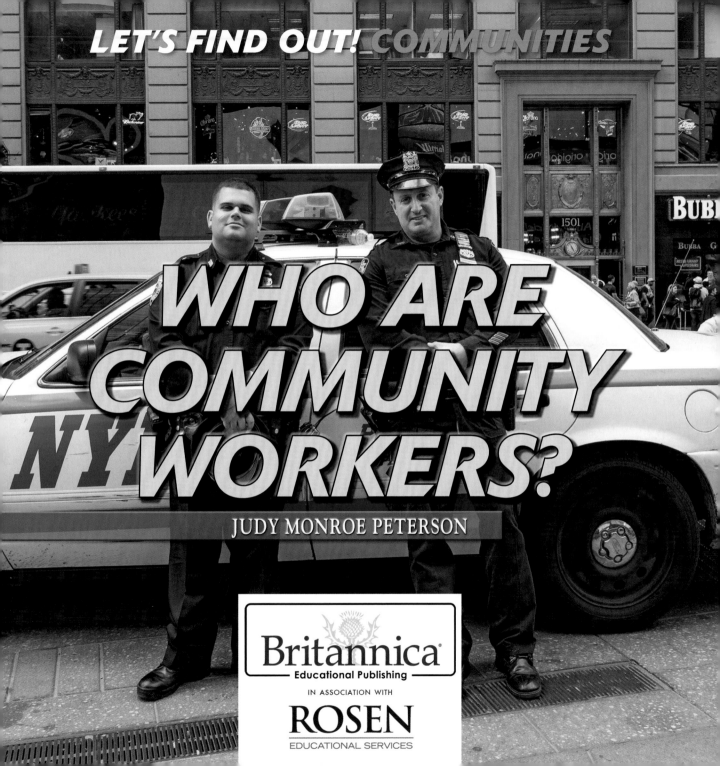

WHO ARE COMMUNITY WORKERS?

JUDY MONROE PETERSON

Britannica®
Educational Publishing

IN ASSOCIATION WITH

ROSEN
EDUCATIONAL SERVICES

Published in 2018 by Britannica Educational Publishing (a trademark of Encyclopædia Britannica, Inc.) in association with The Rosen Publishing Group, Inc.
29 East 21st Street, New York, NY 10010

Distributed exclusively by Rosen Publishing.
To see additional Britannica Educational Publishing titles, go to rosenpublishing.com.

First Edition

Britannica Educational Publishing
J.E. Luebering: Executive Director, Core Editorial
Mary Rose McCudden: Editor, Britannica Student Encyclopedia

Rosen Publishing
Bernadette Davis: Editor
Nelson Sá: Art Director
Matt Cauli: Designer
Ellina Litmanovich: Book Layout
Cindy Reiman: Photography Manager
Sherri Jackson: Photo Researcher

Library of Congress Cataloging-in-Publication Data

Names: Peterson, Judy Monroe, author.
Title: Who are community workers? / Judy Monroe Peterson.
Description: First edition. | New York, NY : Britannica Educational Publishing, 2018. | Series: Let's find out! Communities | Includes bibliographical references and index.
Identifiers: LCCN 2016058551| ISBN 9781680487398 (library bound : alk. paper) | ISBN 9781680487374 (pbk. : alk. paper) | ISBN 9781680487381 (6-pack : alk. paper) Subjects: LCSH: Community life—Juvenile literature. | Human services personnel—Juvenile literature. | Civil service—Juvenile literature. | Communities—Juvenile literature.
Classification: LCC HM761 .P47 2018 | DDC 307—dc23
LC record available at https://lccn.loc.gov/2016058551

Manufactured in the United States of America

CONTENTS

Community Workers

A community is a group of people who have shared interests or who live in the same neighborhood, town, or city. In a community of people who live in same area, there are workers who help all the members of the

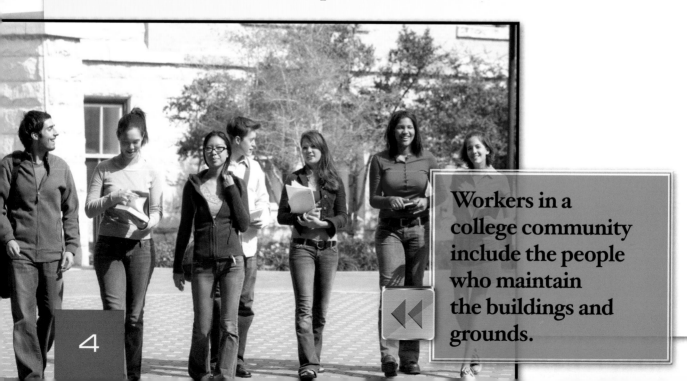

Workers in a college community include the people who maintain the buildings and grounds.

4

Different community workers, like doctors, help community members who need them.

community conduct daily life. The workers have different jobs and responsibilities that keep a place and its people healthy, clean, and safe. Community workers can include doctors, firefighters, police officers, teachers, and government leaders.

Each community has different needs and resources. A large, wealthy city may be able to afford more workers than a small town can. The large city may also need different kinds of workers than a small town does.

COMPARE AND CONTRAST

One city hires many workers to care for its park. Another city can only hire one worker for the same purpose. Why would those two communities have different numbers of workers for their parks?

Doctors and Nurses

Doctors are people who practice medicine. They are educated and trained to prevent illnesses and to heal the sick or wounded. When treating patients, doctors work with many other people, including nurses and therapists.

There are many parts to a doctor's job. Doctors first

Therapists treat the health of patients without using drugs or surgery.

This nurse is examining her patient's health by checking her heartbeat.

need to identify what has made their patient sick or where the pain is. Then they decide on a treatment.

Like doctors, nurses are professionals who take care of people's health. Most nurses work along with doctors in hospitals, clinics, or offices. Some nurses give support and aid to doctors during surgery. Some care mainly for children or the elderly. Others care for patients with mental illnesses. Still other nurses help patients in schools or private homes.

THINK ABOUT IT

Doctors and nurses keep records about patients. How is record keeping important in caring for patients?

DENTISTS

Dentists are doctors who help patients keep their teeth, gums, and mouth healthy. People go to a general dentist to get their teeth cleaned. It is important to have clean teeth to prevent cavities and tooth decay. Dentists clean each tooth with special tools. If they find a cavity, they fill it in so the tooth stays healthy. Dentists take X-rays to find problems inside the teeth or below the gums. They also treat jaw problems and gum disease.

Many dentists who work in communities are general dentists.

This X-ray helped a dentist look for problems in someone's teeth.

They can begin practicing as soon as they graduate from dental school. A small number of dentists become specialists. This means they must go through extra education after dental school. There are nine dental specialties. The specialties include oral surgery (surgery of the mouth and jaw) and orthodontics (straightening teeth and fixing jaw problems).

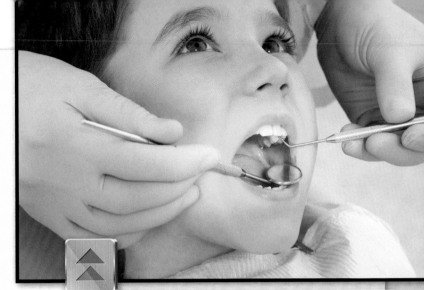

A dentist is inspecting a boy's mouth with special dental tools.

Vocabulary

X-rays are produced using waves of energy. They can show bones in the body.

Veterinarians

Veterinarians are animal doctors. They prevent, diagnose, and treat diseases in animals. They can perform surgery and prescribe drugs, and they also help animals give birth. This branch of medicine is called veterinary medicine. People go to school to become veterinarians. They earn a degree called a doctor of veterinary medicine. Many

This cat has been brought to a veterinarian for a checkup.

Veterinarians at zoos care for tigers and other animals in captivity.

veterinarians work in hospitals or clinics. Others start their own business, or practice.

Veterinarians can specialize in different areas. For example, some only take care of pets. Others are great help in communities with zoos and farms. This is especially important because many endangered animals live in zoos and are in danger of disappearing forever. And farmers can go out of business if a disease kills many of their animals.

THINK ABOUT IT

Why is it important for pet owners to take their pets to a veterinarian for regular checkups?

POLICE OFFICERS

The police are people whose job is to make sure that citizens follow the law and do not harm others. Police officers work for the governments of towns, cities, counties, states, and countries. The police have many tasks. They patrol, or keep watch over, streets and neighborhoods. They do that by car, foot, horseback, motorcycle, or bicycle. Police also go to the scenes of crimes and emergencies to catch criminals

These police are investigating an outdoor crime scene.

Police are trained to use devices such as stun guns as an alternative to shooting a suspect.

and to help victims and survivors. Some police investigate, or study, crimes to find out who committed them.

Some police wear uniforms. Others work in everyday clothing. Many police officers carry handcuffs, a notebook, and a two-way radio. Some also carry a handgun, but they can use a stun gun or pepper spray to stop criminals without seriously harming them. Some officers travel with specially trained police dogs.

COMPARE AND CONTRAST

Is it quicker for a police officer to reach a crime scene in the country or in a city? What might cause this difference in time?

FIREFIGHTERS

Firefighters are trained to control and put out fires. Some firefighters also investigate the cause of a fire to determine if it is arson. Teams of firefighters work quickly to keep fires from spreading. In cities, they connect hoses to fire hydrants and operate pumps to power the hoses to help control fires. In small towns or out in the countryside there are no hydrants. In these areas,

These firemen are working together to control the fire hose and put out the fire.

People who escape a fire often receive medical attention in an ambulance.

firefighters use tanker trucks to bring water to the scene. In addition to putting out fires, firefighters may need to rescue people trapped inside burning buildings. Firefighters also respond to nonfire emergencies, such as road accidents and medical emergencies.

Some firefighter positions require medical training. For these positions, firefighters need to be certified as emergency medical technicians. In many small towns, firefighters are volunteers. That means they are not paid. In cities, firefighting is a regular job.

THINK ABOUT IT

Why is it important for firefighters to work in teams?

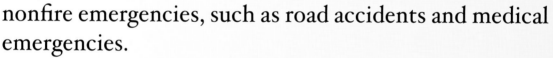

TEACHERS

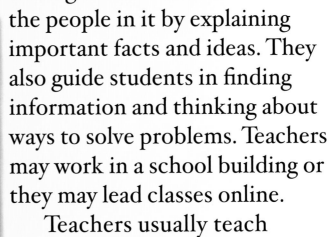

A teacher is someone who educates others for a living. The main job of teachers is to encourage learning. They help students learn new things about the world and the people in it by explaining important facts and ideas. They also guide students in finding information and thinking about ways to solve problems. Teachers may work in a school building or they may lead classes online.

Teachers usually teach students in particular age ranges. In the United States the main

Teachers work with young people to help them learn information and skills.

This professor is giving a talk to students in a university class.

ranges are: elementary (ages five to ten or eleven), middle (eleven to thirteen or fourteen), secondary (fourteen to eighteen), and college and university (adults). Teachers of young children teach all subjects. As students get older, teachers tend to specialize in specific subjects. All teachers inspire students to become educated and successful members of communities.

VOCABULARY

A **university** is a more advanced school than high school. It grants degrees in the arts and sciences and special fields, such as law or medicine.

Construction Workers

Construction workers build or fix houses, schools, office buildings, roads, and bridges. They perform heavy physical labor and often work outdoors in all types of weather conditions.

Some construction workers have particular skills. Concrete workers pour concrete foundations, glaziers deal with glass windows, and ironworkers install iron and steel beams and columns. Electricians, plumbers, and carpenters all work on different parts of a building.

These construction workers are surveying land for a project.

This digger is reshaping a plot of land so builders can make an even foundation.

Other construction workers have more general duties. They are known as construction laborers or helpers. Sometimes workers use bulldozers, trucks, and diggers (also called backhoes) to move dirt to prepare construction sites and to make roads. They may operate cranes to load and unload building materials.

Safety is always important at construction sites because many of the jobs are dangerous. Workers wear safety glasses to keep dirt and debris out of the eyes. Hard hats protect heads from falling objects. Ear plugs protect the hearing of workers who use loud equipment.

VOCABULARY

Debris is something broken down or destroyed.

Transportation Workers

Transportation workers include truck drivers, railroad operators, and ship workers. They may transport raw materials, such as food, minerals, and wood, to factories where the materials are made into products. Other workers then use trucks, railroads, or ships to move the products, such as clothes, shoes, and furniture, from factories to stores.

People in some communities also rely on transportation workers to get them to their jobs or to school. Bus

This shipyard worker is removing protective wrapping from a boat. Boats require regular maintenance.

and streetcar drivers and subway and train operators provide public transportation throughout big cities. School bus drivers safely deliver students to school. Other transportation workers in communities regularly collect and haul away garbage and recyclables in trucks. Airplane and jet pilots can quickly move cargo and mail and fly people to vacation spots and to visit family and friends.

Bus drivers are responsible for the safety of the children they transport.

POSTAL WORKERS

A postal service is a system used to send mail (letters and packages) from one place to another. People mail their letters and packages by placing them in a mailbox or taking them directly to the post office. Postal workers sort the mail according to its destination (the place where it is going). They may sort it by hand or with the help of machines. Postal workers tie sorted mail in bundles and put it into sturdy sacks. These sacks are marked with the mail's destination. Postal workers send the mail to its

Postal workers like this man sort packages by destination.

Some post offices process passports so that people can travel to different countries.

destination by truck, train, ship, or airplane. Postal services around the world cooperate so that mail can even travel between countries. At the destination, letter carriers deliver the mail to each address. Many letter carriers travel on foot or in small mail trucks.

COMPARE AND CONTRAST

Heavier mail costs more to send than lighter mail. Why is this true?

Federal and State Government Leaders

The United States has several layers of government. The national government (also called the federal government) oversees the whole country. Leaders in the federal government do many things. They defend the country from outside enemies, keep order within the country, and provide services for its people.

The federal system has three separate branches

The House and Senate work to pass bills in the Capitol Building in Washington, DC.

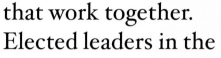

Washoe County Courthouse in Reno, Nevada, belongs to the county government.

that work together. Elected leaders in the legislative branch make laws. An elected president is the head of the executive branch, which carries out laws. The judicial branch interprets laws through courts.

Each state also has its own government. State governments are organized much like the federal government. The people of each state elect a governor and other leaders to run the state. Each state has a court system as well. State government leaders must decide how to pay for services such as education and health care, as well as for the building of roads, bridges, and other projects.

THINK ABOUT IT

Laws limit the powers of federal and state leaders. Why is this important?

City and Town Government Leaders

Like countries and states, towns and cities have a government. A city government usually includes a group of elected lawmakers called the city council. In some cities the people also elect a leader called a mayor. In other cities the city council names a leader called a city manager.

The powers of a mayor or city manager are determined by the law. Some

In 1967, Carl Burton Stokes became the first African American mayor of Cleveland, Ohio.

VOCABULARY

To **manage** is to look after and make decisions about something.

mayors are so powerful that they may actually run the city. They enforce laws, **manage** public services, and oversee city budgets and projects. In other cases a mayor leads the city council but cannot act on his or her own. Sometimes mayors act mainly as a symbol of the city, while the city council holds most of the power.

The leaders of city governments manage many community services. These include police protection, firefighting, and hospitals.

Mayor Bill de Blasio of New York City at a local football game.

COMMUNITY VOLUNTEERS

Volunteers are people who spend some of their free time helping others in the community. They do not get paid for their work. Volunteers may help families who have lost their homes, clothing, food, and other things after a flood, hurricane, or earthquake. Some people volunteer to protect animals or the environment or to coach sports teams.

Young people can volunteer in their

People often volunteer with others to do such things as picking up trash in a park.

Volunteers at a food bank sort and pack groceries to give to the needy.

communities in many ways. They might pick up trash in their neighborhood or in a park. They might also collect canned food for a local food bank. Volunteering can involve walking a dog, raking leaves, or shoveling snow for a neighbor who is elderly or ill. Volunteers often plant and water flowers or vegetables or pull weeds at a school, neighborhood, or community garden. Schools often need volunteers to help run booths at events. Volunteers are important members of any community.

THINK ABOUT IT

Why do many firefighters in towns and cities serve as volunteers?

Glossary

carpenter A worker who builds or repairs wooden structures.

cement The fine powder that is one of the main ingredients of concrete, a man-made stone.

city council Elected officials who work with the mayor to set laws and run the community.

city manager A person hired by the city council to run a city.

emergency A situation that calls for immediate action that would otherwise result in a large amount of harm or loss.

government A group of people that makes laws and runs a community.

ironworker A worker who makes heavy iron or steel products.

mayor An elected official who acts as a head of a city or town.

medicine The science that deals with the prevention, cure, or easing of disease.

patient A person under medical care and treatment.

plumber A worker who puts in or repairs the pipes and fixtures that support the distribution and disposal of water.

rural Of or relating to the country, country people or life, or agriculture.

survivor A person who stays alive after an emergency has ended.

therapist A person trained in methods of treatment other than the use of drugs or surgery.

treatment An attempt at healing someone who is sick or wounded.

urban Of or relating to the city, or a thing that is from the city.

For More Information

Books

Arnold, Tedd. *Firefighters*. St. Louis, MO: Turtleback Books, 2014.

Bellisario, Gina. *Let's Meet a Teacher*. Brookfield CT: Millbrook Press Trade, 2013.

Bellisario, Gina. *Let's Meet a Veterinarian*. Brookfield CT: Millbrook Press Trade, 2013.

Scarry, Richard. *Richard Scarry's Busiest People Ever!* New York, NY: Golden Books, 2017.

Waldendorf, Kurt. *Hooray for Construction Workers!* (Bumba Books ™ — Hooray for Community Helpers!). New York, NY: Lerner Publications, 2016.

Websites

Because of the changing nature of internet links, Rosen Publishing has developed an online list of websites related to the subject of this book. This site is updated regularly. Please use this link to access the list:

http://www.rosenlinks.com/LFO/workers

INDEX